A Bee Is

By Liza Charlesworth

ISBN: 978-1-339-02782-1

Art Director: Tannaz Fassihi; Designer: Tanya Chernyak
Photos © Getty Images and Shutterstock.com.
Copyright © Liza Charlesworth. All rights reserved. Published by Scholastic Inc.

1 2 3 4 5 6 7 8 9 10   68   32 31 30 29 28 27 26 25 24 23

Printed in Jiaxing, China. First printing, August 2023.

SCHOLASTIC

A bee is not mean.
A bee is a neat bug.
We need bees a lot!

See the bee on the leaf.
It has wings and six legs.
It can flap! It can creep!

See the bee on a rose.
The bee drinks from it.
Sip, sip, sip!

Bees meet in a hive
to make sweet honey.
They are a team!

queen bee

Can you spot the queen?
She has a dot on her back.
She leads the bees.

Trees and crops need bees.
Bees make them big.
Bees make them green.

See the wax, cream, and treats.
We need bees to make
each of these things.
A bee is such a neat bug!